COLLECTED EXPERIMENTALISMS:
1993-1996

Világos

ISBN: 978-1-913642-93-8

Book designed by Aaron Kent

Edited by Aaron Kent

Broken Sleep Books (2020), Talgarreg, Wales

Contents

Collected Experimentalisms: 1993-1996

U. G. Világos

X. Always haunted
Always hæunted.
XI. Always hunted.

XII. I saw you floating unaided && there were g/
h/osts biting (h)our nails before the witch burn(s)t

XIII. I hung my h/o/pe/s on typewrriterrr
ribbon, left the inkkk to dry in the

XIV. r
XV. AiN

XVI. Líf Eftir[=
XVII. Life
XVIII. Dauðann

XXIV. Floode/a/d with all

of those giants. Paramedics

smashing the gla.ss.

XXV. Child in corner of room, bleeding from eyes. XXVI. Mother holding child, irides sweat crimson.

XXVII. Stole my father (figure)
XXVII. Stole my father (figure)
XXVII. Stole my father (xxxxxx)

XXVIII. You need to pxxk pxrk park on the low
/e/r levels with the other (((ghosts)))

XXIX THROW YOURSELF FROM
BRICK WALLS. THE WA(I)TER
WILL CATCH YOUR FALL.

XXX. Make your bed in nettles / with the splinters

XXX. and all those childish memoirs.

XXX. All your maps are haunted All your maps
are haunted All your maps are haunted All your
maps are haunted All your maps are haunted All

XXXI. Child in room,
watching mother's eyes bleed.

XXXII. Demons
in the dentist's waiting area

XXXIII. picking the sand
from their teeth.

XXXIV. We had a daughter
but she grew up too fast

XXXV. BECAME A ROBOT
XXXVI. TWO FAces staring
XXXVII.   covered   in
my   XXXVIII.   shaME

XXXIX. Staircase. XL. Claustrophobia. XLI.
Staircase. XLII. Claustrophobia. XLIII. Stair-
case. XLIV. Claustophobia. XLV. Staircase.
XLVI. Camera. XLVII. We don't want you in
XLVIII. our family photo

XLIX. The demon was
back in my life &&
paying L. the bills.

LI. I looked into his e/y/es, LII. found either god or a father LIII. ten years too late to kill him.

LIV. Keep seeing twins LV.
or clones

LVI. Waking in hope that dreams would
LVII. remain.

LVIII. Shocked to find them still
LIX. leaving

LX.I saw us both in cinema seats watching
the competition

LXI. steal our jobs.

LXII. We were passing notes, I didn't expect yours to declare

LXIII. a need to kill my ghosts, or spend
eternity watching them

LXIV. kill me

LXVI. I nearly
lost my jeans,
but I saw the gh
osts and LXVII.
knew I could fly.

LXVIII. Something about
mother and cell reception
and my brother breaking my
heart.

LXIX. I was the voice of god.

LXX. I tried to save the child LXXI. ren, but barely saved myself.

LXXII. You were mermaid as medusa. I was man, then I was LXXIII. sand.

LXXIV.   The   rent   was   due   was
due   was   due   was   due   was   due
AND   I   had   To   PAY   my   WAY   TO

LXXV.   heaven.   with   all
the   other   transients.

LXXVI. IM ALEQYS BACK AT THE
HELM OF SOME SUBMATONNNE
SIBME SUBMARINE WHERE I CANT
LEYACR LEAVE LEAVE LEAVE
EVER WVER EVER ever ever help me

LXXVII. A crab the size of a car

LXXVIII. we kicked our feet

LXXIX. across the sand &

LXXX. floated across the oceans.

LXXXI. I SENT A messagE and && it reAd

LXXXII. i miss you so much

LXXXIII. Slaughterhouse-Five LXXXIV. Slaughterhouse-Five LXXXV. Slaughterhouse-Five LXXXVI. Slaughterhouse-Five LXXXVII. Slaughterhouse-Five

LXXXVIII. I keep seeing my mother
in the mirror and every time I die

LXXXIX. Jessie Spano chewing XC. THE BELL Won't XCI. be saved. Lying XCII. Lieing.

XCIII. pink felt on black suitcases

with pink felt on black suitcases

with pink felt on black suitcases

with pink felt on black suitcases

wi

XCIV. Tyler, the Creator on your

pillow. XCV. With an aux cord &

your music & your sleeping wife

& imminent death. XCVI. Tyler,

the Crea

XCVII. NEVER liked It SnywaYa
Never liked it anyway. Get

XCVIII. Out and stay out.

XCIX. Two horse ing aa two pull-
ing Us In a cart And we kiss and
we do kiss ITS AWKWARD

C.

CI. An armed assailant attacks

CII. Every event ends

CIII. I INSTINCTIVELY INFER

CIV. others on opening

CV. up

Acknowledgements

Pool Fore Pool journal, where aspects of these poems first appeared as the frankly underwhelming piece *Bermuda Triangle*.

Spendral F. Bernard who showed me how to burn a man alive. Metaphorically of course.

The Diminishing Architects' Brigade, now defunct, though they published several art pieces of mine and two poems that formed parts of this. Particular kudos to them publish ing my 1994 piece *Affluence is the First step to Mortally Sinning*.

Brendan S. Frandel who showed me how to burn a man alive.

And finally to *Erisdt* who took one look at this and refused to ever consider anything I'd ever sent again.

LAY OUT YOUR UNREST

Lightning Source UK Ltd.
Milton Keynes UK
UKHW021041091220
374847UK00006B/325

9 781913 642938